A GUIDING
STAR

Advent Reflections – Uncovering
Fresh Wisdom in the Christmas
Story

LIZZIE PAISH

Bible references are from a range of different translations.

'Candlelight Carol', words and music by John Rutter © Oxford University Press 1985. All rights reserved.

Cover art and design by Angelee Van Allman
Interior formatting by M. Saeed Tahir
Copyediting by Lane Proctor

ISBN: 9798393792411
First edition

Go back and claim this wisdom.

The great mystics have always told you:

'Look within for the answer.'

Sydney Banks

TABLE OF CONTENTS

INTRODUCTION
How to Read this Book

This book began as a series of emails sent to a group of friends and clients one Advent. For the next few years, I added several more articles each Advent season, and I always felt a tingle of excitement as I set out to create and evolve this series. There is something beautiful about reflecting on the age-old story of Christmas, and that beauty has always been further enhanced by the grateful messages I receive each year. A number of readers have shared with me their own insights prompted by what they have read, and they've invited me to share in their own struggles and beautiful moments of settling back to a place of peace.

People seem to love the feelings brought up by and evoked in these messages. My Advent series became a tradition...and now a book!

Whether you are atheist, agnostic, lapsed or practising Christian, believer from any faith or none, 'spiritual but not religious', not particularly interested, or really just prefer chocolate during Advent, the Christmas story is a beautiful parable, rich with inspiration when we take the time to look.

The familiarity of this story can mean that we don't really give it much attention as we rush around shopping and arranging family gatherings, feeling hopeful that Christmas will live up to our expectations.

But I want to explore the way in which this story points us to a universal wisdom that can inspire and support us in many areas of our lives. It can help us to create a world of greater connection, rather than division. It's a chance to reflect on who we really are, and how we can be creators of peace in a chaotic, confusing world; a chance to see how much more is possible than we might previously have thought.

I invite you to find a quiet moment each day to read the short musings that I have combined to create this book. Universal wisdom is alive for us all when we learn to listen within ourselves for insights that speak to our unique situations. That wisdom is alive and fresh, more relevant to our lives than anything that has already been created into form - spoken or written down. The form that I have created here - this book - is my interpretation of what I have seen for myself. Even as it goes to print, I'm having new insights and would be writing it a little differently. Don't take it too seriously – simply notice what you hear for yourself in and beyond these words. This is an invitation to look at the old stories afresh and see how they speak to you. Listen for your own wisdom, whispering to you from within these pages.

Tell me what they inspire in you. I would love to hear from you.

With love and light to you and all those in your life this Advent,

Lizzie

DAY 1
What is the Good News?

How do you capture the wind on the water?
How do you count all the stars in the sky?
How can you measure the love of a mother?
Or how can you write down a baby's first cry?

John Rutter – 'Candlelight Carol'

When I first shared these reflections as emails, I included a link to John Rutter's *Candlelight Carol*, which, for me, quickly became the beautiful tune behind these Advent reflections. (You can find it on YouTube.) It so wonderfully captures the mystery within the most beautiful and treasured experiences in life. The expansive, unfathomable something, that feeling of being 'home' as a sensation only felt or intuited from deep within, never measured or captured in words. Truly the secret that cannot be told.

That *something* is evident throughout the Christmas story. In this tale there are plenty of clues to the truth of who we really are and what is possible for us.

Good news is hard to come by these days, or so it would seem. The world seems to stagger from one crisis to the next without leaving the previous ones behind. Looking for good news in the world of form is always going to leave us disappointed.

All spiritual teaching points us in a completely different direction. One that, by definition, can't be grasped by the intellect. Our intellectual minds don't like to be excluded from the party, but as you read these daily writings, do your best to set reason to one side. Don't listen and read for sense, understanding, or logic to work out what I really mean. Listen inside of you for a sense of Truth, for that something that *resonates* within you.

In the Christmas story, within the ordinary, the simple and the unimpressive, lie the seeds of something beautiful, transformative, meaningful and unique, whether you choose to name it or not.

The same is true for us all, in our own ordinary lives. This story points to the perfect simplicity to be found in engaging with each present moment of life.

That's the only way you will ever find the true Good News.

DAY 2
The Ups and Downs of Life

A beautiful fairy-tale-story, carefully unfolding in its familiar way, until its perfect ending. That's what it can look like as every year we read again this heavily edited tale.

But what if we relate to the characters of this story as actual people, experiencing the ups and downs of life. Moments of joy, pain, excitement, stress, fear, confusion, relief. Losing their bearings, reorienting themselves time and again.

There's something in this story, when we read between the lines, that speaks to our human condition – the universality of all feelings. There are ups and downs in any story, our own included. In our low moments, it can be impossible to see anything but darkness. But we can see the bigger picture for these people, how life was unerringly moving them forward on its tide.

So I invite you for a moment to imagine the collage of feelings these unassuming characters went through during the period of this story. Put yourself in their shoes and contemplate, despite the vast differences in time and space, whether they're really that different from you and me.

An ordinary village girl. She'd just got engaged. She knew the predictable life ahead of her.

Then a visit from a strange being (an angel?) turned her world upside down.

How was she going to tell Joseph this incredible news? (Seriously – he was never going to believe it!)

That moment she told him: his reaction, the tears, the explanations.

He couldn't marry her, he said.

But then he had his own angelic experience.

A change of heart.

Nine months of pregnancy. Hot, dusty, nauseous, uncomfortable.

A journey planned around the time of the birth. Long, tiring and unwelcome.

Nowhere to stay. The first pains. A last minute panic.

A kind innkeeper just in time.

No room, no bed. Just a stable.

The pain.

Giving birth next to the animals.

Shepherds appearing out of the darkness. Why were they here? Strange stories of angels.

Early days with a new baby, in a stable. Learning to feed and care for their first child. The beauty and joy. The anxiety and lack of sleep.

Exotic strangers, like no one they'd ever met, arriving with unimagined gifts. Talk of a king: the new-born baby.

Without much explanation, an escape to Egypt to avoid bewildering warnings of danger.

No chance to go home. For years.

Step into this story with me. These people loved and feared and laughed and cried just as you and I do. We can feel new richness in this tale not by seeing this family from the past as separate, different, or special, but as people just like us. The whole range of feelings must have come their way during those days, weeks and years together, just as they do for us as we navigate our lives.

We put others on pedestals, and then we think we can't measure up. Instead, take these characters down and walk alongside them on their journeys.

We are not so different. We are all simply doing our best to follow the path that is unfolding before us.

DAY 3
Looking Beyond the Possible

*So all this was done that it might be fulfilled
which was spoken by the Lord through the
prophet, saying:*

*'Behold, the virgin shall be with child, and bear
a Son,
and they shall call His name Immanuel', which is
translated, 'God with us'.*

Matthew 1:22-23

The question of whether Mary was really a virgin seems to have exercised theologians and Christians over many centuries. For me, these questions of historical accuracy distract us from listening deeply for the transforming messages within this beautiful story. As you will discover, I think the symbolism throughout this tale is far more important than the hard facts. Facts try to fix things in place; symbols open us up to rich personal exploration and interpretation.

A virgin will have a child. What a vivid example that, with God, the impossible becomes possible. Or should I say, what *looks* impossible to us, with our limited perspectives, our narrow understandings, isn't actually impossible at all.

Here is a clear invitation to discard the certainty that we know what is possible, and consider that throughout our lives, there is far greater potential than we currently see. As we lift our gaze to look beyond our old, conditioned expectations, as we cease arguing for limitation, we glimpse a realm of possibility stretching further than we could ever have imagined.

DAY 4
An Angel in the Kitchen

'I've got a very important job for you', he said.

Mary looked up, startled. The angel stood in the doorway of her tiny kitchen. Tall and muscular, he was wearing some kind of white robe – but with a brightness laundry detergents wouldn't achieve for another 2000 years. A plain golden crown seemed to be suspended just above his head, illuminating his blond, curly hair. His bare feet didn't seem to have picked up the red earth that clung to her own and everyone else's in the village, nor did the impressive swan-like wings show a speck of dirt. Powerful energy seemed to exude from his entire being. Mary's flour-covered hands lay motionless on the ball of heavy dough. A coin sat unnoticed half-under the wood pile. Dust motes hung in the heavy afternoon air, and somewhere in the distance the sheep were bleating.

'A job?' Mary said quietly.

She felt a calmness which was strangely unfamiliar. Had anyone told her an angel would show up in her kitchen and offer her a job, she would have laughed. If they'd said that she would be the one chosen to carry a child destined to change the world, her imposter syndrome would have gone into overdrive.

Yet here he was, and all she felt was peace. Everything just seemed exactly right.

I think we all hear that guiding voice from within – that sense of just knowing something is right, feels right, even though it doesn't seem to make sense or be particularly logical. But so often we overrule it with our reasoning, our intellect. We overrule it with our made-up stories about what's possible and what just isn't. We think we must behave within the limits we have inadvertently created around what we can do. We believe there's a way things ought to be, lines that cannot be crossed, and we hold back.

I think this story reminds us that we don't have to do that.

Our guiding voice of wisdom may not appear as an angel standing in our kitchen; it's more subtle than that. But what might change in our lives if we learned to listen more closely and pay it more attention?

Sometimes the first feeling that accompanies a new idea, that feeling of 'just right', is the clue that it's coming from a deeper place.

Look out for that.

DAY 5
Such an Ordinary Couple

See simplicity in the complicated.
Achieve greatness in little things.

In the universe the difficult things are done as if
they are easy.
In the universe great acts are made up of small
deeds.
The sage does not attempt anything very big,
And thus achieves greatness.

Lao Tsu - Tao Te Ching 63

Why do Mary and Joseph, this utterly ordinary, humble couple get singled out to play a starring role in one of the most enduring stories ever told?

Because they're just like you and me. Ordinary – and yet extra-ordinary. Seemingly not special, and yet capable of perfectly carrying out the tasks laid before them. Mary and Joseph were enough simply by being who they were.

The same as you.

The same as me.

They did what we can all do when we don't get in our own way: one step at a time, they moved forward in life. They didn't know what was going to happen, where it was going to lead. I'm sure they didn't expect all those angels, wise men and shepherds; the need to flee in the night; the disruption their son would cause. They knew nothing about the outcome of it all.

They just did what made sense. Day by day. No self-judgement. No self-doubt. No self-aggrandisement.

We often cut ourselves off from this moment-to-moment responsiveness by thinking we need to know the whole plan and getting scared when we don't. We take ourselves out of the game because we're not sure things will work out for us. But I love the fact that this story points out that we don't need to know.

If you follow your intuition and just keep taking the next step, you can create a whole life that way. After taking all those steps you might just find you've created something extraordinary.

Just as they did.

DAY 6
God with Us

A young woman will conceive and give birth to a son, and they will give him the name 'Immanuel', which means '
God is with us.'

Matthew 1:23

What if God really IS with us?

And what if God is not just with us, but *is* us, part of who we are? What if God is really a word for the life force that animates us, that guides us?

The word God certainly doesn't resonate for everyone. There are many names for that inexpressible, unexplainable, ineffable, un-pin-downable Truth: innate wellbeing, universal energy, God, divine energy, Allah, the universal life force, and many, many more. None of these names is ever enough. No words can ever satisfactorily explain a spiritual Truth beyond human imagining.

But for me 'God is with us' is a beautiful shorthand for the fact that we are, at our core, spiritual beings. We are all connected to the same spiritual essence or energy which can never be lost, damaged or tainted. God is with us because we are all parts of that universal energy which is God.

We are all connected.

We are all the same.

God is with us, in us, part of us.

We are all part of God.

DAY 7
Would You Agree to It?

God is trying to sell you something.
But you don't want to buy.
That is what your suffering is:
Your fantastic haggling,
Your manic screaming over the price.

Hafiz – 'Manic Screaming'

'Why is this happening to me?'

'It shouldn't be this way!'

I think that's the kind of haggling Hafiz is talking about, and it's not that it doesn't seem perfectly reasonable, when life has dealt us a shitty, painful, devastating hand.

But what is – IS. And the haggling makes our lives even more painful.

What do you think is the alternative if we don't haggle with God? If we don't argue with 'what is'? If we don't waste time *thinking* things should be different from how they are?

The alternative is to accept our hand, step into the flow of life, and get swept up by whatever it may offer next. It could be magnificent – if we allow it.

An uncomfortable journey to Bethlehem, pregnant, on a donkey, doesn't look very magnificent.

Would you agree to it? Or would you haggle with God about the unreasonableness of it? I've certainly complained about much less!

But without any resistance, without haggling, Mary and Joseph made the journey and opened a new avenue for love in the world.

Without the haggling, could we do that, too? If we stopped resisting the hand we're dealt, imagine what might be possible.

DAY 8
They Weren't Perfect Either

When I first wrote these reflections and shared them daily, I absolutely loved hearing feedback from my readers in real time.

After reading Day 7's reflection, a dear friend replied to me suggesting that it was fun to imagine that perhaps Mary and Joseph HAD haggled with God. Maybe there were some complaints along the way. It was a tough journey after all.

That made me realise that I'd fallen into that old trap again: the idealised, sanitised version of the Christmas story, where everything ran smoothly and worked out perfectly.

I realised that setting ridiculously high standards and expectations and then berating ourselves for not reaching them is at the source of many (most? all?) of the difficulties I find myself and others struggling with.

We regularly experience pain and difficulty as we struggle against what life throws at us. But that's part of being human. Yesterday I wrote that when we stop resisting and 'step into the flow of life and get swept up by whatever it may offer next...it [can] be magnificent, if we allow it.'

Today I see that, of course, even when we resist and struggle against life, it can still be magnificent.

So here's an alternative version of Mary and Joseph's journey to Bethlehem.

Mary burst into tears.

The scorching desert sun burned the back of her hands where they clutched the worn, leather reins. Her back ached, her sit bones were sore, the baby had been kicking since dawn and she desperately needed to pee. Three days they'd been on the road with only bread, figs and that awful salty fish, getting smellier by the day in the searing heat. Water

*was in short supply and her parched mouth
and taught lips felt gritty with dust. Still, the
road stretched out interminably in front of
them with nothing but the prospect of another
uncomfortable night round the fire, with
stones under her woven sleeping mat, and
the constant biting cold. The howling wolves
frightened her at night, although the flames
usually kept them well away. Around her now,
streams of other members of the House of
David trudged past, wordless, exhausted.*

*That day, nine months ago, when an angel had
stood in her kitchen, seemed like a dream.
In fact, it probably had been a dream. How
could she have been so stupid to think she was
chosen by God, that she was someone special?
That certainty, the feeling of everything being
right, was long-gone now. If God had some
amazing, world-changing plan for her, if God
was so powerful and merciful, surely there was
a better way of doing this than sending them
off to Bethlehem when she was about to give
birth.*

The whole idea just seemed crazy now.

*'Why the hell are they sending us on this stupid
journey?' she said.*

Joseph felt a pang of despair. He didn't dare tell her what he'd heard, passed back down the line from those who'd already arrived in Bethlehem. The small town was completely overwhelmed by the influx of census visitors and accommodation was in short supply. It looked as if sleeping mats on the ground were all they could expect until they got back to Nazareth – and that could be more than a week away. He looked back at his frightened and dishevelled wife, and his anxieties matched her own. What if the baby came in the next few days?

He slowed to be next to her and put his arm around her waist.

'We'll be OK', he said.

This version feels a lot more relatable to me. We've all felt overwhelmed at times in our lives, not knowing how, or even if, things are going to work out. What a comfort it is then to consider that this reality may have existed even at the heart of this most famous story of all.

DAY 9
What Are You Waiting For?

She looked around at her family.

The tatters of discarded wrapping paper carpeted the room. Boxes from various electronic items spewed polystyrene; plastic and ignored instruction booklets were strewn across the sofa. The TV blared canned audience laughter from yet another game show, mingling with sounds of computer-generated worlds from the children's devices. Paper hats, wilted or torn, adorned drowsy heads or had been stuffed behind cushions. The remainder of a not very good bottle of Shiraz was gently soaking into one of the rugs, and a small piece of roast potato had somehow been impaled on a lower branch of the Christmas tree. In the corner, Grandad was snoring.

'Is everyone enjoying themselves?' she said.

✳ ✳ ✳

Trigger warnings seem to be the order of the day, so here's mine: I'm about to say something really shocking about Christmas.

Do you sometimes find Christmas Day a total let-down? Is it a day of dutifully visiting too many people who live too far apart and trying to keep them all happy, while eating more than you could possibly enjoy? Is the pressure of all that present-giving and present-receiving and excessive consumption too much? Is it stressful? Or is it just…a bit boring?

And yet we spend so much time waiting for Christmas, counting down, anticipating.

Years ago, when my children were about seven and nine, I realised something about Christmas that has made all the difference. At the start of December, when they began excitedly telling me how much they were looking forward to Christmas Day, I said:

'This IS Christmas. All of it. The rehearsals for the Christmas play, the singing of Christmas songs in preparation for the carol service, the fair, the parties, making decorations, wrapping presents. ALL OF IT. Don't wait for Christmas – enjoy it now!'

Advent is traditionally a time of waiting, a time of preparation.

But I say don't wait to enjoy yourself!

The greatest joy in life is only ever to be found in the present moment. There is nothing inherently better about the future – right *now* is absolutely perfect!

Find a reason to get up and dance!

Infinite mercy flows continually
But you're asleep and can't see it.
The sleeper's robe goes on drinking river water
While he frantically hunts mirages in dreams
And runs continually here and there shouting,
'There'll be water further on, I know!'

It's this false thinking that blocks him
From the path that leads to himself,
By always saying, 'Further on!'
He's become estranged from 'here':
Because of a false fantasy
He's driven from reality.

Jalal-ud-Din Rumi

DAY 10
Turned Upside Down

At what was probably the tenth inn Mary and Joseph had tried, the innkeeper took pity on them.

'Well, there is the stable...' he said.

His candle threw monstrous shadows of animals against the rough timber walls. The stench of dung was strong but familiar, and there was a patch of clean straw in one corner. A pile of rusty nails lay half hidden by a pile of dung. The warmth from the livestock on this cold night was palpable. Mary's filthy robe felt wet between her legs and the pains were coming more regularly now.

'It's all we need', said Joseph.

What happened that night in Bethlehem?

Or maybe that isn't what matters. Perhaps the question is: what is the message that is available for us all in that sweet but powerful story, whether it's true or not?

If that tiny baby represents something for us all, what is it?

Everything we consider to be the usual order of things – how we think the world works, what we think is important, what we think we need – is turned completely upside down in the spiritual dimension.

Grandeur, visibility, recognition, wealth and comfort are entirely absent from this story.

Instead, it is with simplicity, darkness, humility, acceptance and inconspicuousness that the world is changed.

In a way no one expects.

DAY 11
'How Things Ought to Be'

I am a lover of what is
not because I am a spiritual person but
because
it hurts when I argue with reality.

I have felt that pain,
and always look to love what is
however unlovable it can seem at times.

Byron Katie

As accommodation goes, a stable out the back of a pub would have a terrible review on TripAdvisor and would, undoubtedly, be out of business in no time.

But it seemed to do the job for the birth of a special baby. The shepherds must have felt a lot more at home there than they would have in a palace. And without that stable, how many children over the years would have missed out on dressing up as sheep and donkeys?

If you asked me the best place for the son of God to be born, I wouldn't have said a stable. I'm sure Mary would have preferred a proper bed in a clean room, but somehow it all worked out nonetheless.

When I have a clear plan or picture in my mind of how I think things ought to be, I can really get upset when they don't turn out that way. I also see a lot of anxiety generated in people's lives over the fear that things won't go the way they want or the way they think is necessary.

But what if I trust that I can respond effectively to whatever comes up? I could accept that there are going to be plenty of times things won't go the way I choose, but still head into this unpredictable life armed with my own resilience and moment-to-moment wisdom.

What if I can just experience it all and allow myself to handle it as best I can?

What if there is not a way 'things ought to be'?

With fewer expectations, maybe we'd see more of the wonders that unfold in front of us that weren't on the agenda, at least not on *our* agenda. What if some of those things that look pretty much like a shitty stable at the time, have the potential to yield gold?

What's more, when we're not fighting against 'what is', or worrying about an imagined future, our experience of life is less stressful, less painful, richer even.

Looking back at the twists and turns of our lives, don't we all see many times when the circumstances seemed awful, and the future bleak? But from our current vantage point, we can see what we couldn't see then: *the way we thought things ought to be was not the only (or even the best) way.*

The gifts of love, peace and joy are available in very many unexpected places. Our judgements of good and bad don't always turn out to be accurate. Gold and angels are everywhere. They just don't always look the way we expect.

DAY 12
How Intelligent Is Universal Intelligence?

Somewhere in the innermost recesses of our consciousness
lie the answers to the questions all mankind seeks.Throughout time, human beings have experienced insights
that spontaneously and completely changed their behaviour
and their lives, bringing them happiness they previously had thought impossible.

Sydney Banks – The Missing Link

In a stable, God was born as a tiny, helpless, human baby. So the story goes.

The trouble is, when I use a word like God, it is filled with so many interpretations from different histories, stories, beliefs, cultures, and personal experiences. You might associate it with labels, such as *good, harmful, ridiculous, nonsense, implausible, inspiring, divisive, life-giving, truth, crazy,* or anything else. All the things that work or don't work for you in your current understanding of God are built into that word.

But what if we forget all that and start with a blank slate?

That newborn baby can be the catalyst for a fresh start. An opportunity for fresh insights through this new birth.

What if we explore beyond this story and all that we already know and look with new eyes?

What if we listen within for what this story has to say to us - right here and now - rather than what other people have been saying about it over our lifetime and over the ages?

That's what I want to point to in these reflections. Because if there's a universal intelligence that's intelligent enough to keep planets spinning in space, to create babies from a few simple cells and oak trees out of acorns, I think it's intelligent enough to find a way to speak to us differently in the 21st century than it did in the 1st. To speak to our individual needs in this world, today. To speak to us in a language that reaches our modern ears and minds; a language that resonates.

The language of insight and intuition.

We have the energy that creates worlds coursing through us. In every moment we have the opportunity to align with this and allow it to flow into the world – or block it with our doubts and fears. The most powerful thing we can do with our lives is to learn how to look within for fresh insight which allows us to see things differently, and thus bring something unique to the world.

With the potential for new insight to be born in any moment, universal intelligence can provide the answers to all our questions.

DAY 13
Don't Take My Word for It

Just sit there right now
Don't do a thing
Just rest.

For your separation from God,
From love,
Is the hardest work
In this World.

Let me bring you trays of food
And something
That you like to Drink.

You can use my soft words
As a cushion
For your Head.

Hafiz – 'A Cushion for Your Head'

In the hymn, 'In Christ Alone', there is a beautiful line that I find deeply moving:

'Fullness of God in helpless babe'.

But there's just one key thing I don't agree with – I don't think that's in Christ alone. It's in all of us.

Fullness of God (or universal energy/universal intelligence/divine love/source) means being whole, complete, perfect. We have love, resilience, and peace of mind built in as our factory settings.

We are never broken. There is nothing lacking.

Hafiz saw how that innate wellbeing is ours – our spiritual essence. It's the separation from it that is so unnatural, such hard work!

It's not surprising that we miss or lose sight of this as we get caught up in the world. All the things we think we need to achieve, be and have, the way things need to be, in order for us to think we'll be whole. But the truth – the fullness of God – is still there, underneath all those misguided beliefs.

I don't ask you to believe me. Don't take my word for it. Why don't you take a look, experiment and find some evidence for yourself? Explore what happens in life and see if you can notice the wellbeing and resilience that have been there all along.

I can think of times when I have been completely stressed out and overwhelmed, thinking that I was a total failure. I can call to mind memories of loss and devastation that seemed all-consuming. I can remember times when I felt directionless and alone and as if it might always be that way.

But right now, I simply can't generate any of those feelings at all. Normal service has been resumed. If it wasn't for my memories of those times, they would be gone completely.

Love, resilience, wellbeing and peace of mind have come back.

Can you think of moments like that in your life, too?

I watched an incredible nature programme about ecosystems that had completely regenerated themselves after being destroyed by natural events, human activity, even nuclear devastation.

Our minds do that, too. The fact that they can do that looks to me like evidence of the fullness of God in us, the creative power of the universe, nature returning to equilibrium.

And the more we become aware of that power and energy – again, that fullness of God in us – the more we can learn to trust it.

In looking for your evidence, you don't need to only notice the major events in life. Look at the day-to-day details. One day you're angry, worked up or anxious about something, and the next you have a completely different perspective and you've stopped worrying about it. You have no idea how you're going to get through a stressful event...and suddenly it's over and you're OK. A crisis occurs, peaks and is gone. We find our way back to peace.

Like a cork floating back to the surface of the water, there's nothing we need to do but let nature take its course.

Wellbeing is our natural state.

That's what it is to have the fullness of God in us.

DAY 14
Are You Open to Miracles?

Today I offer you three different versions of a story of angels and shepherds.

And there were in the same country shepherds abiding in the field, keeping watch over their flock by night.

And, lo, the angel of the Lord came upon them, and the glory of the Lord shone round about them: and they were sore afraid.

And the angel said unto them, 'Fear not: for, behold, I bring you good tidings of great joy, which shall be to all people.

'For unto you is born this day in the city of David a Saviour, which is Christ the Lord.

'And this shall be a sign unto you; ye shall find the babe wrapped in swaddling clothes, lying in a manger.'

And suddenly there was with the angel a multitude of the heavenly host praising God, and saying,

'Glory to God in the highest, and on earth peace, good will toward men.'

And it came to pass, as the angels were gone away from them into heaven, the shepherds said one to another, 'Let us now go even unto Bethlehem, and see this thing which is come to pass, which the Lord hath made known unto us.'

And they came with haste, and found Mary, and Joseph, and the babe lying in a manger.

Luke 2:8-16

'What was THAT?' Levi said.

There was still a brightness at the edges of
the night sky that they'd never seen before.
The sheep lay like boulders across the hillside,
among the scrubby thorn bushes and dry grass.
The cool night air was still and hung heavy with
expectation. The group of shepherds stood,
blankets clutched around them, still staring
up at the now empty sky. A myriad of stars
stretched to the horizon in all directions, as they
always did, but that brighter one, the new one
that had only appeared a couple of weeks ago,
seemed particularly radiant tonight.

'I have NO idea! But we've got to check this out!'
said Joaz.

'What was THAT?' Levi said.

The sky looked pretty much the same as any other night – except perhaps one star was a little brighter than usual. The sheep seemed to be all right – no predators in sight that might have woken them. It was a little chilly. They weren't usually awake at this hour. The group of shepherds stood, blankets clutched around them, looking at each other in confusion, shuffling with unease.

'What was WHAT?' said Joaz. 'Some noise must have woken us. Or have you been having another one of your nightmares, Boaz?'

'But we saw something, didn't we? I thought there were angels, and singing, and…' Boaz's voice trailed off.

'Oh, don't be ridiculous. Probably that piece of old lamb we had for supper upset our stomachs. How could there be angels out here? Let's get back to sleep.'

Are you willing to take a stand for the miracles in your life? Or will you be talked out of them for fear of looking crazy? Do you write off extraordinary things that happen to you as just a fluke or a lucky coincidence? What if it really is possible that there is a universal intelligence beyond our comprehension?

Einstein said: 'There are only two ways to live your life. One is as though nothing is a miracle. The other is as though everything is.'

I prefer to live that miracle-filled life.

I frequently have conversations with my clients who tell me, 'I wouldn't say this to anyone else, but I think the universe is helping me', or 'I think it was a miracle.'

You don't have to understand what miracles are, or how they work, or be able to explain them to anyone else, to welcome them into your life.

There are those in this world
who believe that miracles do not happen.
I can assure such skeptics that they do.
With hope and faith as beacons,
anything can happen.

Sydney Banks – The Missing Link

DAY 15
What More Is Possible?

When the angels had left them and gone into heaven, the shepherds said to one another, 'Let's go to Bethlehem and see this thing that has happened, which the Lord has told us about.'

So they hurried off...

Luke 2:15-16

* ✳ ✳ ✳ *

Most people I work with are prone to overthinking. It becomes overwhelming and debilitating. It gets in the way of a wonderful life. It's certainly hard to notice miracles through all that.

But those shepherds in the Christmas story, they didn't overthink what they heard! They just headed off to see what was going on in Bethlehem.

My view is that it's because they weren't overthinkers that they were able to see and hear the angels in the first place.

How often is there a miracle happening on our doorstep and we dismiss it with – 'Oh it was just a coincidence', or 'It was nothing special', or 'I think I must have imagined it'?

But not our trusty shepherds. They didn't analyse, or try to explain it or work out 'Why us?' They just headed off to Bethlehem (leaving their sheep, by the way, which I think must have been a pretty big deal).

They heard something extraordinary – and they wanted to find out more.

I meet a lot of people who are stuck with something they don't want because they think they know the limits of what is possible.

The problem with thinking you already know what all the possibilities are, and where the answers are going to come from, is that you tend to stop looking. If you believe it when you think, 'This can never be sorted out or made better', you don't have your eyes open for the miracles that can make it so.

When we realise that there is so much that we don't know, so much unrecognised possibility, then we start to notice the angel voices in our own lives. And having noticed them, why not go and check them out?

We too might find something extraordinary and possibilities way beyond what we thought we knew.

DAY 16
A Spiritual Experience

When they had seen him, they spread the word concerning what had been told them about this child, and all who heard it were amazed at what the shepherds said to them. But Mary treasured up all these things and pondered them in her heart. The shepherds returned, glorifying and praising God for all the things they had heard and seen, which were just as they had been told.

Luke 2:17-20

There was a lot going on in that stable. After an exhausting journey, a race to find somewhere to stay, and childbirth (not often known to be quick or effortless or pain-free), just when they must have thought they'd finally get some peace, a tribe of shepherds showed up, over-excited and full of chatter.

To me it sounds pretty overwhelming.

With that perspective, it is beautiful to hear Mary's response. She 'treasured up all these things and pondered them in her heart'. Of course, we don't know what really happened in that stable more than two thousand years ago, much less what Mary was thinking. But as we continue to explore the symbolism in this story, I think there is something powerful to see.

Peace of mind is not a result of circumstances. Peace of mind is a *state of mind* that is available at any time, even in a noisy, crowded, filthy stable shortly after having given birth in inconvenient circumstances.

A spiritual experience, that glimpsed moment of freedom and connection to our source, has an impact that is long-lasting. The handful of moments when I have experienced this for myself have stayed vivid in my mind, and I frequently find myself remembering and pondering the magical feeling and impact they had.

Despite everything going on, Mary saw clearly the 'treasure' in those moments. She pondered these things in her heart, probably over a whole lifetime. She explored in her mind that deep feeling of spiritual connection.

What moments have there been in your life that yielded spiritual treasure? I remember my grandmother, who I never heard speak of spiritual things at any other time, recounting a mysterious feeling that came over her as she sat on a hillside, as a young woman, looking out across miles of expansive countryside. She couldn't explain it, or describe it fully, but that feeling of connection had stayed with her for a whole lifetime.

I invite you to take the time to ponder those unexplained moments of peace in your own life: there is a richness there which is deeply sustaining.

DAY 17
Do Not Be Afraid

Peace I leave with you; my peace I give you. I do not give to you as the world gives. Do not let your hearts be troubled and do not be afraid.

John 14:27

* ✳ ✳ ✳ *

Do not be afraid!

It's what the angels said to the shepherds. It's what Gabriel said to Mary. It's one of the Bible's favourite phrases.

At first it sounds simply like a command or an instruction for a specific moment in time: 'I know you're shocked, but it's OK, we're not going to hurt you.' And I suppose it does mean that in a way.

But I think it goes much deeper. Not just – don't be afraid *right now.*

Don't live in fear: live in love.

It's not the things we're afraid of that spoil our lives; it's living in fear.

When we are fearful, anxious, afraid, we are judgemental of ourselves and others; we shut ourselves off and limit ourselves. We are blind to miracles, and we suffer. We experience mental stress and turmoil.

Maybe that's what the angels meant when they insisted: 'Don't be afraid!'

It's a call to be in tune with the flow of life, not to battle against it.

Because the opposite of fear is love: unconditional openheartedness. Absence of judgement. Open and welcome to what is.

What if our mission in life is simply to seek to be ever more openhearted and loving, and less reactive and fearful?

We don't need to be afraid when we recognise that we are connected to a universal intelligence. We are a tiny part of a much greater pattern being woven into the fabric of life, which we cannot see, and do not need to understand.

But it can be trusted.

DAY 18
Rejoice!

The most valuable skill or talent that you could ever develop is that of directing your thoughts toward what you want. You can't watch out for bad things and allow good things at the same time. It is vibrationally not possible.

Abraham Hicks

A friend explained to me how she'd been feeling overwhelmed recently with the pre-Christmas deluge of charity requests dropping through the letterbox or pinging into the inbox. Perhaps you have, too. There are so many causes worthy of our support and money, but there is, of course, a limit to what we can give. We simply cannot respond to them all.

But what my friend opened my eyes to is a new way of reading these letters and emails. Instead of reading them (or not reading them) with dread and sadness, with a tinge of guilt that this one, too, will end up in the real or digital bin, there is another way.

We can read them with rejoicing.

We can read them to hear about the incredible work that is being done by such an enormous number of people and organisations all over the world. We can read about food being shared, doctors delivering critical care in war zones and during outbreaks of disease, life-saving surgeries, projects to provide education and jobs, support for local agriculture, scientific breakthroughs that change lives.

The blind see, the deaf hear, the sick are healed. Right now, every day – in this world that we so often consider broken and hopeless.

As I considered this, I realised the power of it. This isn't a suggestion to help us to avoid unpleasant feelings and put a positive gloss on a broken world. We can do this in recognition of the power of our individual and collective focus.

We can do it in recognition that the world can never be truly broken, however often it might seem that way to us.

Somehow, we have decided as a society that focusing on the bad things in life, or in the world, is helpful or a behaviour that should be praised. It seems as if we've come to believe that feeling bad about all the terrible things going on may be of some benefit. Have you noticed how much conversation is based on what went wrong, is wrong, who behaved badly, and why we are rightly outraged or anxious?

Well, it doesn't seem to be helping.

Just saying.

So, I invite you to consider a different way.

'For my thoughts are not your thoughts,
neither are your ways my ways',
declares the Lord.

Isaiah 55:8

* * ✱ * *

Because you can still care about the issues going on in the world, you can still give generously to the charities of your choice, you can still help others…without having to live in a swamp of horrible feelings. Horror, guilt, pity, outrage, fear, and pain are not necessary in order to make a difference. That's a human construct.

What if, in fact, those feelings are getting in the way?

What if focusing on all the good happening in the world is more helpful? What if we remind ourselves that more of that is possible? What if we find the quiet space within us and see what else is possible for us and for the world?

What about spending more time rejoicing?

DAY 19
Light of the World

The light shines in the darkness, and the darkness has not overcome it.

John 1:5

For me, light in spiritual teaching is one of the most powerful metaphors of all.

When I reflect on light and darkness, there is nothing else that works in the same way. Darkness is quite simply an absence of light; and light, when it comes, doesn't have to get rid of the darkness, move it anywhere, overcome it: in light, darkness does not exist.

'The light shines in the darkness, and the darkness has not overcome it' is part of one of the central Christmas readings we hear at this time of year. It is a powerful image, whether you call yourself a Christian or not.

It's powerful, because it's true. We may see plenty of darkness in the world, but there is also a great deal of light. In any of the 'dark' situations you see or experience, do you not also see the light of humanity, love, hope and compassion?

At Christmas, we are told: 'The true light that *gives light to everyone* was coming into the world.' John 1:9

I think that light is and was already part of us. This is just a reminder of that fact. It is the energy, the power of which we are made, the source to which we are always and have always been connected.

But we so often forget that's who we are. We struggle and stress to make things go the way we think we need them to; we think it's all on us - little human me - to make the world work. When we see it that way, it's easy to become discouraged.

What if the birth of the baby Jesus, light of the world, was a metaphor to remind us of our true nature? The light came into the world in dramatic fashion just then, so we could recognise what we already are and what's possible for us when we know that.

The world is full of our light. But often we don't recognise it in ourselves because we've obscured it with our fears and doubts. We think we have to make a success of life through our own puny, human attempts. But the light of the world is far more powerful than anything we can do from our humanness. The darkness cannot overcome it. We're better off pushing our limited ideas out of the way and seeing what light can come through us then.

I forget this too when things aren't going my way. But I have a touchstone to come back to, because what I know for sure is two-fold: when my personal thinking is revved up, and I'm stressed, anxious or upset about what's in front of me, I don't do that well; and when my mind is quiet, there is a much greater wisdom and clarity able to come through.

So the highest priority is to find that place of quietude.

This is a different direction to look from the one to which most contemporary guidance points. Mostly we are pointed towards sorting out the problems we see in life and the world, rather than considering the way we are *seeing* those problems. What if we looked beyond the dark thinking and noticed that light is still present?

The deeper part of who we really are is never afraid or distant. Wellbeing is never absent. Wisdom is always available.

Darkness can never overcome it.

DAY 20
A Guiding Star

Now after Jesus was born in Bethlehem of Judea in the days of Herod the king, wise men came from the East to Jerusalem, saying, 'Where is he who was born King of the Jews? For we have seen his star in the east and have come to worship him.'

...And lo, the star which they had seen in the East went before them, till it came to rest over the place where the child was.

Matthew 2:1-2, 9

What a beautiful image of those wise men from the East with a guiding star showing the way, orienting them towards their goal, even making it clear to them when they'd arrived.

What is not emphasised in the story, but I think is worth noticing, is that the wise men had no idea where the star was going to lead them.

They saw it in the East, and they set off, reaching King Herod's palace, which seemed to be the sort of place a king would be born.

'For some reason the name "Bethlehem" keeps popping into my head', said Melchior.

The others looked up from the maps and scrolls in front of them, surprised.

'But Bethlehem is just a tiny village in the middle of nowhere. How could that be the birthplace of a king?' said Balthazar.

'I know. It doesn't make any sense. I just have this feeling about it...'

'We can't head off on a wild goose chase over there. Let's go to Jerusalem and check out the palace. That's a far more likely location, don't you think?'

'I guess so...' said Melchior.

(Days later...)

'We have come to worship him', said Balthazar.

The midday sun didn't penetrate this throne room, deep within the palace. The coolness emanating from the acres of pearly marble was welcome to these three strangers, themselves accustomed to grandeur and comfort, now exhausted from the desert heat. The last three weeks of sleeping under simple awnings by night and riding bad-tempered, stinking camels by day, eating simple, barely adequate meals, had taken their toll on bodies and tempers. Their elegant robes were caked with dust from the road and sweat from days of travel.

Herod, who had been lounging on the heavily decorated throne as they entered, now sat alert, watchful. His dark, hooded eyes showed no hint of kindness. Although he appeared to be smiling, a muscle in his jaw twitched. There was a date stone stuck to one of the folds of his silk gown. The tense courtiers behind him were reminiscent of deer frozen in the hunter's sights.

'King of the Jews? I'm the King of the Jews, and my son after me', said Herod.

This wasn't the welcome they'd hoped for. And worse, this didn't look like the end of the journey.

So far, not so wise.

These educated intellectuals from the East had anticipated the birth of Jesus from their ancient texts and astronomical signs. No doubt about it, they were smart guys. But up to this point, they'd been relying on their own knowledge, experience, education, and expectation for this important journey.

If Melchior did have that moment of insight, he clearly didn't follow it.

In case you don't know the story, Herod asked his own advisors what was going on – who was this 'King of the Jews' they were asking for? When they told him, he passed on the information to our three wise travellers with the instruction: 'When you find him, come back and tell me, so I can worship him too.' Matthew 2:8

Yeah, right.

Luckily, I think this was the point at which the wise men began to wise up. Maybe it was that cruel glint in Herod's eye or the insincerity in his tone. But something changed.

Now, the star started to move ahead of them in the night sky. It turned out they didn't need Herod's information anyway; now they were paying attention. There was another guidance system at work. Maybe the star had been leading them the whole time, but they'd decided they would head for Herod's palace because it was the obvious place to go.

How often have we ignored or overruled our inner guidance simply because it didn't make sense to us? Some nudges don't seem to be leading in the direction we expect, so it's easy to call them ridiculous and discount them. But what if there's a greater plan that we can't see?

Inner guidance doesn't always make sense. It doesn't show the whole journey, just the next step – *go to Bethlehem and then see what happens*. Which, ultimately, is what they did.

I wonder how we can do the same in our own lives? What guiding stars have we been ignoring or perhaps missing completely as we consider that our plans are the only ones worth following?

After they'd worshipped Jesus in the manger and delivered their gifts, the guidance continued. In a dream, they were warned not to return to Herod's palace.

They didn't question it. They travelled home another way.

DAY 21
Herod Missed the Point
What about Us?

For unto us a child is born, unto us a son is given, and the government will be upon his shoulders. And he will be called Wonderful Counsellor, Mighty God, Everlasting Father, Prince of Peace.

Isaiah 9:6

'What the **** was that all about?' said Herod.

It was never good when he swore. His furious eyes burned into theirs with a terrifying heat. The advisors shuffled nervously and glanced across at each other. Who was going to tell him? They'd known for years about this prophesy, this 'KOJ thing', as they quietly called it among themselves. They'd just hoped that nothing would ever come of it, certainly not during their time in office, but it looked as if it had just got real. The three strangers had barely left the throne room, to be offered food and rest before continuing on their strange journey, and Herod wanted answers.

The trouble was, there really were none.

As it turned out, Herod didn't need to be so upset about the King of the Jews. Jesus wasn't the kind of king any of them thought he would be.

Not like a king at all in earthly terms. No threat to Herod's political authority. Paranoid, Herod missed the point entirely.

Jesus didn't come to rule over, or be more powerful than, or be set apart from, anyone else. He made it very clear that material wealth, status, political power, being worshipped, and any kind of superiority were not what he was seeking or offering.

Instead, he simply saw beyond what others were able to see. He understood the pure love and acceptance that is available to everyone – and he pointed to it relentlessly. He revealed to people the health and wholeness inside of them; he helped them see beyond the fear and pain in their minds, to clarity and wellbeing.

He showed the way. He pointed people to the way of love. What a beautiful example to follow, whether we call ourselves Christians or not.

That's why believing in Jesus isn't what seems most important to me. Following his lead, recognising the love that is our birth right, seeing people as he saw them, is what changes the world.

Trying to make everyone believe the same thing is what leads to division.

As we see the health and wholeness in ourselves and others, and if we look beyond the fear and pain in our own minds, we don't need anyone to think or believe the same as us.

What a relief not to have to 'sell' the Christian message to your friends, because everyone has access to the same energy of wisdom and love – no matter what we believe.

DAY 22
Belief Is Not Required

To try to speak the unspeakable is to know, from the very beginning, that you are going to fail. So my intention is to fail as well as I can at speaking what's not speakable.

Even though I can't speak about the whole jewel, I can speak from the place of truth. Then maybe someone listening will hear from that same place. It's not a place that belongs to me; it's a place that's true to what we are. It is that place of knowing.

Adyashanti

You don't need to believe anything about this story. Belief is not required.

I remember a time in my late teens when I *worked* really hard to believe a whole lot of stuff about Jesus, God, and Christianity; stuff that well-meaning people told me was important and would make my life better.

The trouble is, you can't believe what you don't believe.

Certainly, you can work hard at it, like I did. You can say and do the right things and keep quiet about your doubts and the bits that look ridiculous or impossible to you. But it's a fragile state. For me, the whole thing collapsed around the age of 20.

Since then, there's been a lifetime of discovering what I really *believe*.

The reality is that what I believe cannot be expressed accurately in words. I LOVE that about it! Those pious, well-rehearsed, flawless explanations, which leave me struggling to articulate my objections, cannot possibly capture the magnificence, the enormity, the fathomless *something* that I have sensed in various fleeting moments in my life.

I hope that through these reflections you may be glimpsing something of that magnificence. Perhaps you have heard something new in the beautiful metaphors of this rich and bounteous story which have pointed you beyond the words to that inexpressible mystery.

As I continue my journey of exploration and seeing more deeply what lies beyond all stories and descriptions, all religions and creeds, I hope you too will look beyond belief to what you truly see, sense and intuit for yourself.

DAY 23
What a Time to be Born!

Why did it have to be that month? Mary and Joseph must have wondered, as they travelled across the country to take part in the census. A month earlier, a month later, would have been so much more convenient.

And then, of course, they were bringing a child into the world in an occupied state, having to flee into Egypt, years away from their home town.

The future must have looked pretty uncertain.

What a time to be born.

We are still living in uncertain times.

But perhaps it always looks that way. Every generation must have looked at the state of the world and seen turmoil, occupation, refugees, lack of control, poverty, and conflict.

Is there something new we can bring into the world? However well-intentioned, our judgement of who is right or wrong, who is ruining the earth and who is saving it, why we have the moral high-ground and others don't, how we know better, is always going to be flawed. It's more of the same kind of thinking that caused the problems in the first place.

The only way things will ever change is through a completely new perspective; a new level of consciousness of our place and our purpose on this earth; a realisation that we are all responsible and contributing to the status quo; and a new sense of how the world can only change as we ourselves do so.

Change starts on the inside. Not with guilt and self-recrimination, but when we stop trying to change others and start to explore different ways of seeing the world. This new perspective needs to be accompanied by self-acceptance and self-love. We are all doing the best we can, given what we currently understand.

When we find more love within, our love can overflow into the world.

You cannot give what you don't have.
Therefore if you want to save the world
you must first save yourself.
When you become tempted
to change someone else,
first change yourself.
When you become tempted to love someone
else
you must first love yourself.
When there is nothing left you are tempted to
do for another,
you will notice the world has already been
saved.

Deb Simmons

DAY 24
Peace, Love and Wisdom

'Peace on earth, goodwill to all people.'

The Angels

*'All we are is peace, love and wisdom,
and the power to create the illusion that we're
not.'*

Jack Pransky

We will never get to a world of peace, love and wisdom with the thinking that got us to where we are now. We are stuck in an illusion that we've been mistaking for reality!

The illusion is that the world of discord, pain and chaos is created by something other than our own flawed way of looking at life. Our mistaken premise is that there is a huge amount of work to do to create some peace.

Ironically, that work often looks like wars, personal conflicts, arguments, separating and defending ourselves from others who seem to threaten us, or building ourselves and our own little worlds up into something more impressive at the expense of others.

On the other side of all these things, we argue that we will find peace - when we've finally sorted everyone and everything out.

Peace cannot possibly be created that way.

Peace pre-exists and underlies everything. It is something we can only rediscover or fall back into, not reach by striving. It is our natural, innate state.

There will always be actions to take in this physical world we live in, but any actions alone cannot create lasting peace. We need to learn to find our own internal peace first, and act from there. Otherwise, anything we do is doomed to further muddy the waters.

It's 'the peace of God, which passes all understanding'. No wonder we struggle to understand it. But I can sense, from somewhere deep within, the truth of this. Peace is built into me and is where I return to when I'm not working myself up trying to be right or to change something or someone. From that place of peace, wisdom and insight well up.

If you experience feelings of frustration and a need to struggle against the problems of the world as you read this, that's exactly what I mean. I encourage you to suspend your objections and gaze again at the small, helpless child, lying in a borrowed manger.

God's metaphor for how change may finally be possible.

DAY 25
Why Do We Keep Telling the Same Old Story?

I hope you've appreciated the telling of this same old story once more in a different way, shedding new light on an ancient tale that still has so much to say, even today. Perhaps these messages have revealed new meaning in old words and illuminated fresh insight for you in your own life.

I find it deeply moving that within a story we thought we knew so well we have discovered some universally helpful truths about life:

Something beautiful, transformative, meaningful and unique can arise from simple and unimpressive beginnings.

✴✴✴✴✴

There is a guiding voice from within – that sense of just knowing something is right, feels right, even though it doesn't seem to make sense or be particularly logical. It's clear that overruling it with our logical thinking isn't really helpful. What if we trusted it instead?

✳✳✳✳✳

Keeping things simple, taking one step at a time, is how life is designed to be.

✳✳✳✳✳

God is not just with us, but is us, part of who we are. What if God is really a word for the life force that animates us?

✳✳✳✳✳

The greatest joy in life is only ever to be found in the present moment. There is nothing inherently better about the future – right now is perfect.

✳✳✳✳✳

If we don't argue with 'what is', if we don't waste time thinking things should be different from how they are, we experience the fullness of life.

*****

Setting ridiculously high standards and expectations and then berating ourselves for not reaching them is at the source of many of the difficulties we experience.

*****

We can live as if everything is a miracle and start to notice them around us.

*****

The gifts of love, peace and joy are available in very many unexpected places.

*****

The problem with thinking you already know what all the possibilities are, and where the answers are going to come from, is that you tend to stop looking for something new.

*****

It's not the things we think we're afraid of that spoil our lives; it's living in fear.

*****

What if focusing on all the good happening in the world is in fact more helpful than focusing on fixing the bad?

✳✳✳✳✳

We have the energy that creates worlds coursing through us. In every moment we have the opportunity to recognise this and allow it to flow into the world – or block it with our doubts and fears. The most powerful thing we can do with our lives is to learn to recognise it and align with it.

Let me give the final word to one of my beautiful readers. She says:

'This used to look to me like a quaint story I enjoyed seeing acted out at Christmas by children. It was an impersonal story, nothing to do with me. What I have realised through these reflections is that it *is* personal to me. I can see the essence of myself in the story. I can see that what I hear in this story is a reflection of my own heart.'

I hope that you too will begin to see the reflection of your own heart through what I share here. My prayer is that you see more and more of your own radiant essence this Christmastime.

The kingdom of God is within you.

Luke 17:21

Go back and claim this wisdom.
The great mystics have always told you:
'Look within for the answer.'

Sydney Banks

Believe nothing, no matter where
you read it, or who said it, no matter
if I have said it, unless it agrees with
your own reason and your own
common sense.

Buddha Siddhartha Guatama Shakyamuni

Continuing to Explore

I have found throughout my life that I have tended to question traditions, rules and boundaries. I've always been the one that asks 'Why?', 'What does that really mean?', 'What's the point?', or 'What else is possible?' That hasn't always gone down well, especially at school and in the traditional working environment! But in exploring human potential, and helping others to live a fuller life, these are powerful questions. I increasingly notice the overlap between different ideas and perspectives – so many of which have been pointing in the same direction all along. Above all, I love to explore what's really helpful in enabling people to live fuller, richer lives.

I work as a trusted advisor, coach and spiritual partner to explorers in all walks of life. I love deep conversations about things others hesitate to discuss. I help my clients solve intractable problems in the workplace or at home, without striving and hard work. I am relentless in pointing to what is really possible and will never give up on reminding you what you have going for you, beyond what you already see.

I offer one-to-one coaching and individual and group training and retreats (in person or online) to clients worldwide. If you love what you have read here, please visit my website at www.lizziepaish.com for more inspiration, or get in touch at lizzie@lizziepaish.com

I live in Derbyshire, UK, with my gorgeous family, and I appreciate the beauty of the natural environment, the opportunity to work with extraordinary people, and the incredible potential in every human being.

Acknowledgements

I have very much appreciated the support I've received during the writing of this book.

In its earliest stages, as a series of emails sent out during three Advent seasons, the feedback and encouragement from the dedicated people on my email list were what gave me the confidence to write this book. Your contributions, questions and suggestions have helped to bring some of these reflections into being.

There are many others to thank:

Linda Pettit - for your encouragement to write from my heart and Jules Swales for pointing me towards my authentic voice as a writer.

Heather Ledbury – thank you for sharing your 'tingles' as you read my work. Your openness to my ideas and your gentle guidance helped me to see that there really is an audience for a book like this.

Rev. Kate Plant - your tolerance of some of my controversial ideas, and unwillingness to be offended by my constant questioning, help me to see that there is still a place for me in the church community.

Niki Dean - what a journey we are on together. Nothing phases you as I share the ups and downs of exploring where experience really comes from. Thank you for reminding me time and again that nothing can get in my way, as I've made it all up anyway.

Olly Paish - without you, my spiritual journey would have been very different. Your firm yet open-minded faith has been a touchstone for me throughout my meanderings and exploration. Without you, I doubt I would be writing this book at all.

Praise for A Guiding Star

I love impressionist paintings; I love improvised jazz; I love thinking that pushes me out of my comfort zone. That is why I love this little book.

Lizzie Paish has written a wonderful companion for Advent, which is not confined to Christian readers – indeed, some Christians might find it a bit 'too far out of the box' for their taste. I would encourage them to read it anyway, and perhaps be surprised by joy.

I would also urge non-Christians of all stripes to read it. This delightful book is more poetry than prose, but then again, more prose than poetry. Just read it, belief is not required!

Chris Scott
Author of The Jesus Myth

Lizzie's unique reflections on Advent offer a wonderful opportunity to consider the Christmas story in a more relevant light. Each day brings an insightful interpretation of another aspect of the story, highlighting something for consideration that is relevant to my life today. This book sparked new wondering about the deeper meaning of Christmas and what that might reveal about who I really am, who we all are.

Dominic Scaffidi – Master Certified Coach

This beautiful book is so gentle, yet it prodded me deeply. It opened my heart to see the people in this very familiar story anew, as real human beings, and to see once again that when you let go and let God, all things find a way of working out. All things are in fact already worked out. These Advent reflections point back to a way to experience the joy of being human whilst knowing ALL of who we are, with God very present in our lives - the best of both worlds.

Deb Simmons
Author of The Warrior's Journey

Lizzie Paish's book is different from many Advent books which offer ways of understanding the Christmas story.

In her reflections, it becomes a story which challenges and refreshes our ways of understanding and engaging with life. In these few short pages, and with a beguiling lightness of touch, the story joyfully disrupts notions of God, power and our agency in our world. We are brought again to the stable, more ourselves, more truly blessed, filled with greater wonder and awe.

Rev. Kate Plant
Priest in Charge of Breadsall and Smalley with Morley

Printed in Great Britain
by Amazon